D1736561

A TRIBUTE TO MY BELOVED ANIMAL

A Journal to Process Grief & Loss

Katie Lawlor, Psy.D., MIA

ISBN-13:
ISBN-10:

Cover design by: Dustin Kieschnick, Psy.D.
Library of Congress Control Number:
Printed in the United States of America

Contents

Disclaimer & Dedication

To this beautiful community of animal guardians – a heartfelt disclaimer: This journal is not perfect. Far from it.

Despite my best efforts, it has typos, awkward word phrases, and is missing aspects I will undoubtedly think of immediately after I press "publish."

…but this document has sat on my desktop for more than 3 years now, because I was afraid to share something with you that wasn't flawless.

Perhaps this sentiment can serve as our safe haven as we move through our grief. There is no perfect way to grieve, just as there is no perfect way to love.

All we can do in this life is show up for each other in the kindest ways we know how.

This journal is dedicated to those who are searching for the courage to do this, as perfectly imperfect humans.

Introduction

Bereavement, the experience of loss, literally means being torn apart.

With fellow humans, especially loved ones, our relationships are complex; they are full of highs and lows, break-ups and misunderstandings, arguments and hurt feelings.

Our companion animals, however, always seem to make us feel better, even on our worst days. We come to rely on their unconditional devotion, and the purpose and fulfillment they bring into our lives.

The profound bond we share with them thus evokes intense grief when they become sick, go missing, are nearing the end of their lives, and pass away.

I do not believe we ever "move-on" after this loss; rather, we – in time – can live in a way that reflects the love they bestowed on us.

That being said, there can be a tendency to fixate on the details surrounding our animal's passing, particularly if the loss was sudden, unexpected, or traumatic.

This is normal, and I want to validate this entirely. However, what can be helpful to remember is that up until that moment, they LIVED. These are memories we will have forever.

This journal provides a protected space to safeguard your thoughts and feelings. Journaling helps get things out of our heads and off our hearts, providing clarity and healing.

All the prompts in this journal have come from my experience working with those who have lost their beloved animals. They recount the questions you have asked, the painful emotions you have struggled with, and the brokenness you have felt.

As you progress through these pages, every word you write is a tribute to the life you shared with your animal. May you know peace in trusting that you gave them an extraordinary life, right by your side, and that is all they ever wanted.

I hope you will also cultivate gratitude for yourself as you gather the strength to continue.

Finally, please know you are never alone in your grief. I can offer understanding because I have been there myself. Several times.

I am so glad we have found each other.

Katie

✳✳✳

Finding Comfort

Although there are many distinguished theories and models of grieving – with different stages and processes – experts agree that the following symptoms are common, whichever combination and order they appear.

Please know this by no means an exclusive list:

- Shock, disbelief, feeling numb, and denial.

- Sadness, despair, loneliness, and emptiness.

- Guilt, regret, shame, anger, and resentment.

- Anxiety, dread, helplessness, insecurity, and fear.

- Agitation, overstimulation, fatigue, nausea, aches and pains, loss of appetite, night sweats, heart palpitations, feeling faint or lightheaded, insomnia, and lethargy.

Furthermore, our grief journey is not linear. We may feel strong one instant, then absolutely devastated the next.

The first few weeks and months, in particular, can seem surreal.

Engaging in soothing activities can provide temporary reprieves from overwhelming sadness.

Below are some initial questions to guide you through your grieving process. These can help you understand your natural responses to your loss.

Gentle reminder: you can return to your answers at any time, particularly when you are feeling scared and alone.

✳✳✳

Reflection Questions:

What comforts you when you're deep in grief? (these can be material items, activities, rituals, people, places, other animals, thoughts, prayer…).

_____

_____

_____

_____

_____

_____

_____

_____

_____

_____

_____

_____

_____

_____

_____

_____

_____

_____

_____

_____

_____

In which environments do you feel calm? At peace?

_____

_____

_____

_____

_____

_____

_____

_____

_____

_____

_____

_____

_____

_____

_____

_____

_____

_____

_____

_____

_____

_____

_____

What is the most difficult time of day for you? Why is this? Is there anything that could soothe you during these moments?

_____

_____

_____

_____

_____

_____

_____

_____

_____

_____

_____

_____

_____

_____

_____

_____

_____

_____

_____

_____

_____

_____

_____

_____

_____

What has someone said or done that has helped you?

_____

_____

_____

_____

_____

_____

_____

_____

_____

_____

_____

_____

_____

_____

_____

_____

_____

_____

_____

_____

_____

_____

_____

_____

_____

Which aspects of your loss are you finding most difficult?

_____

_____

_____

_____

_____

_____

_____

_____

_____

_____

_____

_____

_____

_____

_____

_____

_____

_____

_____

_____

_____

_____

_____

_____

Who or what reminds you that you are not alone?

_____

_____

_____

_____

_____

_____

_____

_____

_____

_____

_____

_____

_____

_____

_____

_____

_____

_____

_____

_____

_____

_____

_____

_____

Meaning While Grieving

Grief is like falling into a chasm. One day everything is fine, the next the world has fallen out beneath our feet. We become completely lost; life feels meaningless, and if we don't have a reason to climb out, we'll stay trapped.

Finding meaning is our lifeline back into the world.

Following the loss of our animals, it can be hard to find purpose, but making intentional, gradual shifts in our life can instill hope, and the ability to cope with what feels impossible at times.

A gentle place to begin is to be honest with yourself about what you truly care about.

The questions below are written to prompt this reflection.

Reflection Questions:

What do I consider a fulfilling life?

_____

_____

_____

_____

_____

_____

_____

_____

_____

_____

_____

_____

_____

_____

_____

_____

_____

_____

_____

_____

_____

_____

_____

What am I proud of?

_____

_____

_____

_____

_____

_____

_____

_____

_____

_____

_____

_____

_____

_____

_____

_____

_____

_____

_____

_____

_____

_____

_____

_____

_____

Who do I want to become?

_____

_____

_____

_____

_____

_____

_____

_____

_____

_____

_____

_____

_____

_____

_____

_____

_____

_____

_____

_____

_____

_____

_____

_____

What inspires me?

_____

_____

_____

_____

_____

_____

_____

_____

_____

_____

_____

_____

_____

_____

_____

_____

_____

_____

_____

_____

_____

_____

_____

How can I become more conscientious about how I spend my time?

_____

_____

_____

_____

_____

_____

_____

_____

_____

_____

_____

_____

_____

_____

_____

_____

_____

_____

_____

_____

_____

_____

What do I want my legacy to be?

_____

_____

_____

_____

_____

_____

_____

_____

_____

_____

_____

_____

_____

_____

_____

_____

_____

_____

_____

_____

_____

_____

In which spaces can I show up as my authentic self?

_____

_____

_____

_____

_____

_____

_____

_____

_____

_____

_____

_____

_____

_____

_____

_____

_____

_____

_____

_____

_____

_____

_____

_____

Who do I love the most? How do I currently show them? Do they know?

_____

_____

_____

_____

_____

_____

_____

_____

_____

_____

_____

_____

_____

_____

_____

_____

_____

_____

_____

_____

_____

_____

Where do I feel at home?

_____

_____

_____

_____

_____

_____

_____

_____

_____

_____

_____

_____

_____

_____

_____

_____

_____

_____

_____

_____

_____

_____

_____

What gets me out of bed in the morning? (This question is meant to be both practical and existential).

_____

_____

_____

_____

_____

_____

_____

_____

_____

_____

_____

_____

_____

_____

_____

_____

_____

_____

_____

_____

_____

_____

_____

_____

Consider What Your Animal Would Want for You Now

Envisioning the life our animals would wish for us, in the wake of their passing, can soften the sting of their absence.

I believe that they would want the connection and warmth you shared with them to sustain you during these dark and uncertain times. I think they would want you to know what a wonderful life they shared with you.

Take a few moments to give thought to what sentiments they would communicate with you now, if they could.

*****

Reflection Questions:

If your animal could impart their wishes for you, what do you believe they'd share?

_____

_____

_____

_____

_____

_____

_____

_____

_____

_____

_____

_____

_____

_____

_____

_____

_____

_____

_____

_____

_____

What would you say to them in response?

_____

_____

_____

_____

_____

_____

_____

_____

_____

_____

_____

_____

_____

_____

_____

_____

_____

_____

_____

_____

_____

_____

_____

_____

_____

The Passage of Time

Our grief does not end at a certain point after our animal's passing, because our love for them does not end.

Reminders of the life we shared often bring back the heartbreak of our loss – even years later.

These painful feelings aren't a "setback." Rather, they're a reflection that your animal's life was, and remains, interwoven with our own.

Each milestone after the loss of our beloved animals can prompt conflicting thoughts and feelings – leaving us feeling stuck, guilty, or confused about "moving forward" in our lives. We may find birthdays, adoption days, traditions, and other special events bittersweet at best, longing to relive previous celebrations when our animals were present with us.

Perhaps we are hoping to experience the joy and promise of a special occasion, but then are reminded of the emptiness of missing our best friends. We might even feel ashamed or mad at ourselves for being festive in their physical absence.

This is your gentle reminder that you can create a balance between remembering your animal who has died, and living a meaningful and fulfilling life in which you can – and will – smile again.

***

Reflection Questions:

Have you been holding yourself back from feeling joy amid your grief? In what ways?

_____

_____

_____

_____

_____

_____

_____

_____

_____

_____

_____

_____

_____

_____

_____

_____

_____

_____

_____

_____

_____

_____

Are there special occasions you have wanted to celebrate but wouldn't allow yourself? Why not?

_____

_____

_____

_____

_____

_____

_____

_____

_____

_____

_____

_____

_____

_____

_____

_____

_____

_____

_____

_____

_____

During these times, what are the words you are telling yourself?

_____

_____

_____

_____

_____

_____

_____

_____

_____

_____

_____

_____

_____

_____

_____

_____

_____

_____

_____

_____

_____

_____

_____

What do you wish you could give yourself absolute
permission to do?

_____

_____

_____

_____

_____

_____

_____

_____

_____

_____

_____

_____

_____

_____

_____

_____

_____

_____

_____

_____

_____

_____

_____

_____

Acts of Kindness & Coping

Even when we are in the utter depths of grieving, we have so much to offer – when we are ready to.

This is in part because as animal guardians, so much of our personal identity – who we are in our hearts – comes from giving.

It's our love language.

When we do things for ourselves and others, human or animal, we feel a profound sense of purpose.

Below are several ideas for how we can cope by giving, as we navigate the loss of our animals.

Please circle those that resonate with you, or that you might like to try. You can also add your own ideas to these lists.

✻✻✻

o   Plan an activity – something that takes ALL of your attention (so you don't have time to think about your loss, for at least a little while) – an art class, cooking, yoga, hiking, gardening, visiting a museum, a lesson, studying a foreign language…

o   Write a letter to your animal in heaven.

o   Start a new tradition on a day that was meaningful in your animal's life.

o   Donate (money or supplies) to a charitable organization in your animal's name.

o   Sponsor an adoption at your local shelter.

o   Plant a tree or flower in their honor in your garden that you can watch grow in the coming years.

o   Plan a themed dinner where the topic of conversation is memories of your animal.

o   Schedule a gathering or a visit with loved ones during times when you're likely to feel lonely or sad (on their adoption day, birthday, etc.)

o   Stay connected to your support systems, such as spiritual or social groups.

o   Walk / run a 5K for an animal rescue or welfare organization.

o   Attend a pet loss support session through your local SPCA, humane society, or related organization.

o   Leave flowers/a plant, a homemade dish/dessert, bag of coffee, or a note on the porch of a loved one as a surprise gesture.

o   Volunteer an hour of your time for a cause that's special to you.

o Drop off baked goods or snacks at your vet's office or for animal shelter staff.

o Offer to run errands for an elderly neighbor.

o Babysit a friend's children.

o Focus on something you are grateful to yourself for doing. For example, if you are afraid that you will forget the memories you made with your animal, remind yourself of the effort you made in creating them.

o Writing our thoughts on paper is useful because as humans, we tend to ruminate on the worst moments in our lives in an attempt to make sense of them, and / or determine if we could have altered the outcome in some way. This detrimental exercise is futile, and ultimately makes us feel incapable, exhausted, and hopeless. We are however more likely to feel a sense of relief once we have some emotional distance from these beliefs, which writing them down helps provide.

o Reading a book or an article, listening to a podcast, or watching a documentary about someone we admire who has gone through loss can offer new perspectives on surviving, and remind us that we are not alone.

***

Establishing an Enduring Connection to your Companion Animal

Many of us who have lost our beloved animals find it reassuring to incorporate meaningful mementos of their love into our daily lives.

For example, you might make their leash into a belt, their collar into a bracelet, their blanket into a pillow, use their food and water bowls as flowerpots or key holders by the front door, and/or have their ashes, fur, hair, scales, or feathers made into jewelry or glass ornaments.

You also might choose to have an art piece commissioned, or frame your favorite photos, displaying these in prominent areas of your home.

A gentle reminder that tributes do not have to be material in nature.

Perhaps you might light a candle for them every evening, or take a weekly walk at their favorite spot.

You might sit in your garden and admire the scenery around you, spending a few moments reminiscing about memories you made together.

***

Reflection Questions:

How are you honoring your animal?

_____

_____

_____

_____

_____

_____

_____

_____

_____

_____

_____

_____

_____

_____

_____

_____

_____

_____

_____

_____

Are there any remembrances you've seen or heard about that resonate with you? What is special / unique about them?

_____

_____

_____

_____

_____

_____

_____

_____

_____

_____

_____

_____

_____

_____

_____

_____

_____

_____

_____

_____

_____

_____

_____

If you haven't yet but would like to memorialize them in some way, are there any barriers – mental, emotional, financial, physical – getting in the way?

_____

_____

_____

_____

_____

_____

_____

_____

_____

_____

_____

_____

_____

_____

_____

_____

_____

_____

_____

_____

_____

_____

_____

_____

_____

Overcoming Our Fear of Loss

As animal guardians, we have an unceasing desire to love, which typically fills us with contentment and satisfaction.

When they pass, however, it can feel as if they've taken a physical piece of us with them. As a result, we may find ourselves terrified to extend our hearts again, afraid that another loss will stop it from beating entirely.

Understandably, but unhelpfully, many of us attempt to cope with our fears by avoiding situations that elicit them.

Over time, this avoidance can leave us numb in our own skin. We may not even notice this gradual detachment, until we look in the mirror one day and don't recognize the reflection gazing back at us.

If we continue to avoid what we used to love before we lost our animals, we may find ourselves living a halfhearted existence.

***

Reflection Questions:

Awareness

To prevail over what petrifies us most in the wake of our loss, we must first articulate it.

For some of us, this might be a fear of never being able to care about another animal to the same extent. Or perhaps we're scared we'll never be as happy as we were in their presence. Or maybe if we do open our home to a new love, it won't feel the same.

What are you most apprehensive about? Be as specific and detailed as possible.

I ask this because our fears can become so rigid and absolute that we instantly accept them as true and therefore permanent.

_____

_____

_____

_____

_____

_____

_____

_____

_____

_____

_____

_____

Act

Our fears are conjured up by our minds to make reality appear more distressing than it actually is, in a misguided effort to "protect" and distance us, even from what we love.

When we gather the bravery to face them, they begin to fade and disappear. This also allows us to reinvest our time and energy into our healing.

What fear(s) do you want to face?

_____

_____

_____

_____

_____

_____

_____

_____

_____

_____

_____

_____

_____

_____

_____

_____

_____

Reframe

Whenever fear strikes, try to "reframe" it – think about it from a different perspective.

For example, instead of picturing all the "bad things" that could happen in a particular scenario, think of something beneficial that could come out of it.

Even better, what's the best possible outcome that could transpire if you acted despite being scared?

_____

_____

_____

_____

_____

_____

_____

_____

_____

_____

_____

_____

_____

_____

_____

_____

_____

_____

Ask

Despite our efforts to steadily carry on, our fears can be barriers to finding stable footing following our loss.

While fears are not facts, they can serve as clues as to the areas of our life we feel have escaped our grasp, or that we want to examine.

Fears can also be very persistent – it may feel like they won't leave us alone until we have addressed them.

Are there any useful hints your fears may be trying to give you?

Do they point to any parts (roles, relationships, responsibilities, etc.) of your life you want to alter?

_____

_____

_____

_____

_____

_____

_____

_____

_____

_____

_____

_____

_____

If you could say anything to your fears, what would you tell them? (You can use explicit language if you'd like).

_____

_____

_____

_____

_____

_____

_____

_____

_____

_____

_____

_____

_____

_____

_____

_____

_____

_____

_____

_____

_____

_____

What's blocking you from telling your fears to go away?

_____

_____

_____

_____

_____

_____

_____

_____

_____

_____

_____

_____

_____

_____

_____

_____

_____

_____

_____

_____

_____

_____

Can you embrace your fears but refuse to let them control your decision making?

Are there any actions you could take, or behavior patterns you could make, to keep your fears at bay?

_____

_____

_____

_____

_____

_____

_____

_____

_____

_____

_____

_____

_____

_____

_____

_____

_____

_____

_____

_____

_____

_____

Vulnerabilities as Powerful Attributes

Our vulnerabilities can be our greatest attributes, once we realize the power and agency they imbue in us.

The sharp rawness of grief comes from losing the soulmate that – no matter what happened out in the world that day – could fix everything once we were together.

They were our home, and their closeness was a source of safety.

It takes unimaginable courage and determination to be vulnerable in this day and age, given society's harsh and often thoughtless response to bereavement for companion animals.

In truth, however, to be vulnerable is to be brave.

The work of a kind heart is never finished, and thus we must learn how to protect and care for ourselves.

Reflection Questions:

Are there areas in your life where you feel guarded or closed off, but would like to be more vulnerable?

_____

_____

_____

_____

_____

_____

_____

_____

_____

_____

_____

_____

_____

_____

_____

_____

_____

_____

_____

_____

_____

_____

How would it feel to show up in the world as your sincere self?

_____

_____

_____

_____

_____

_____

_____

_____

_____

_____

_____

_____

_____

_____

_____

_____

_____

_____

_____

_____

_____

_____

In what ways could your vulnerabilities be viewed as / be made into strengths?

_____

_____

_____

_____

_____

_____

_____

_____

_____

_____

_____

_____

_____

_____

_____

_____

_____

_____

_____

_____

_____

_____

Who would benefit from you becoming the most authentic version of yourself?

_____

_____

_____

_____

_____

_____

_____

_____

_____

_____

_____

_____

_____

_____

_____

_____

_____

_____

_____

_____

_____

_____

_____

_____

Are there ways you would like to be giving more to others –
human and / or animals – than you are now?

_____

_____

_____

_____

_____

_____

_____

_____

_____

_____

_____

_____

_____

_____

_____

_____

_____

_____

_____

_____

_____

_____

Speak with Those "Who Get It" & Have Experienced Loss Themselves

When we are grieving the passing of our animals, most of us rely on human connection for compassion.

In reaching out, however, we may feel ashamed or isolated due to the enormity of our loss – our entire world has been irrevocably shattered. Dismissive responses we receive from others can impact us in all our life roles – personally and professionally.

Speaking with fellow animal guardians – those "who get it" because they too have experienced their own darkness – can instill in us the promise that there will be moments of light again.

This engagement can also validate that the magnitude of our sorrow is commensurate with the love we shared.

Reflection Questions:

Are you suppressing any dark / frightening / hurting / guilty / shameful feelings because you are afraid of how others might react or think of you?

_____

_____

_____

_____

_____

_____

_____

_____

_____

_____

_____

_____

_____

_____

_____

_____

_____

_____

_____

_____

_____

_____

What would you say out loud to someone, if you were certain you wouldn't be judged, but rather supported?

_____

_____

_____

_____

_____

_____

_____

_____

_____

_____

_____

_____

_____

_____

_____

_____

_____

_____

_____

_____

_____

_____

Communicating Our Grief to Loved Ones

It's entirely healthy and encouraged to share about the loss of your animal, whether it's been a day, a month, or a decade after they've passed.

This preserves their spirit and provides you with a necessary release.

Our natural tendency is to seek comfort from those closest to us. While it would be ideal if our loved ones could provide us with the encouragement and reassurance we need, this is not always the case.

If our grief is met with invalidation or apathy from the humans we love, we may experience embarrassment or despondency – in addition to several other emotions that are not conducive to healing.

Connecting with our family and friends during the grieving process is requisite in secure relationships.

I want to caveat here – and it's very unfortunate – that certain individuals in our life may not be safe to share our grief with. It is important that we surround ourselves with those who are able to support us.

Relating what you are thinking, how you are feeling, and how these thoughts and emotions are influencing your actions provides insight into what you need from others during this time.

Furthermore, it is helpful to understand that our emotions influence our relationships, and our relationships influence our emotions.

Below are prompts to provide you with a clearer comprehension of your interactions with those around you, while identifying where your needs are not being met.

If we feel our loved ones don't understand our grief or are unsupportive:

- Describe the situation – what exactly happened?

_____

_____

_____

_____

_____

_____

_____

_____

_____

_____

_____

_____

_____

_____

_____

_____

_____

_____

_____

_____

_____

_____

_____

What had been my expectations of my loved one?

- How did I expect them to feel?
- What did I expect them to believe/think?
- What did I expect them to do?
- What did I expect them to say?

_____

_____

_____

_____

_____

_____

_____

_____

_____

_____

_____

_____

_____

_____

_____

_____

_____

_____

_____

_____

_____

How did I respond to them in return?

- How was I feeling?
- What was I thinking?
- What did I do?

_____

_____

_____

_____

_____

_____

_____

_____

_____

_____

_____

_____

_____

_____

_____

_____

_____

_____

_____

_____

_____

Evaluating my response:

- Were any of my behaviors and / or actions reactionary (as compared to a measured approach where I felt in control)?
- Was this how I wanted to respond?
- Would I do anything differently if I could?

_____

_____

_____

_____

_____

_____

_____

_____

_____

_____

_____

_____

_____

_____

_____

_____

_____

_____

_____

_____

What did I learn about myself and my loved ones?

- Did any of my beliefs about myself change?
- Did any of my beliefs about them change?

_____

_____

_____

_____

_____

_____

_____

_____

_____

_____

_____

_____

_____

_____

_____

_____

_____

_____

_____

_____

_____

_____

_____

How will I move forward?

- Are there more supportive people I can talk to about the loss of my animal? If yes, whom?
- If a loved one hurts me again – whether intentionally or not – what is my plan for how I will respond?

_____

_____

_____

_____

_____

_____

_____

_____

_____

_____

_____

_____

_____

_____

_____

_____

_____

_____

_____

Living Your Values

When we are not living in accordance with our values – the components of life we believe to be most important and those we hold most dear – we tend to feel unfulfilled or lost.

For example, someone who values their home life, yet is rarely able to spend time with their loved ones and animals due to personal or career demands, is unlikely to be content or inspired.

In the wake of loss, our values can feel fractured and out of reach. Grief can make us forget who we are and what we care about.

Setting aside protected time to contemplate our values can prompt a sincere consideration on our desired roles in life, current time commitments, and objectives. Once we have a greater comprehension of these, we can begin to act with intentionality.

Our values can also guide us in the present moment – the only time any of us have is right now. We need to concentrate on what is within our control, and gently let go of what isn't.

As you respond to the questions below, please remember that your values are yours alone, and there are absolutely no right or wrong answers.

✳✳✳

Reflection Questions:

In what ways have your values – everything that is
paramount to you in this life – felt fractured or out of reach
since your loss?

_____

_____

_____

_____

_____

_____

_____

_____

_____

_____

_____

_____

_____

_____

_____

_____

_____

_____

_____

_____

What barriers are in the way of you living your values? (living in such a way that your values are in line with your actions).

_____

_____

_____

_____

_____

_____

_____

_____

_____

_____

_____

_____

_____

_____

_____

_____

_____

_____

_____

_____

_____

_____

Are there any modifications you would like to make in your life following your loss? (It can be useful to be as specific as possible).

_____

_____

_____

_____

_____

_____

_____

_____

_____

_____

_____

_____

_____

_____

_____

_____

_____

_____

_____

_____

_____

_____

Regrets Versus Guilt

First and foremost, there is no such thing as a life without regrets, because so much of what happens to us is out of our control.

Let me explain...

In the context of loss, the word guilt is often used instead of regret. There is a massively critical distinction grievers must know:

Guilt implies that we did something wrong; that we knew what we were doing was wrong at the time that we did it.

Regret, however, is when we look back after an event, wishing we would have known or done something differently, but not knowing that what we were deciding at that moment we would later deem wrong.

For so of us many who have lost a companion animal, we did what we thought was favorable at the time, only to have regrets due to the unknown variables in play.

Now that we have the proper term, we can understand regret as both an agonizing, aching feeling, and a damaging pattern of thinking in which we constantly replay an event, a response, or a lack of action (something we didn't do but later wish we had).

Regrets can become burdens that interfere with our ability to find peace in the present, cause us anguish about the past, and adversely influence our future behaviors.

Regrets cause the wounds of heartbreak to remain unhealed.

If we find ourselves overcome by regrets in the context of our loss, asking the following questions can provide clarity and stability.

Reflection Questions:

"Could I have acted any differently considering the information, knowledge, time, support, experience, and financial resources I had access to at that time?"

If you were to ask yourself this question, you may realize that you did the best you could in the situation, given the specific circumstances and unseen factors.

"Was it only me, or did anything or anyone else contribute to the outcome?"

Those who are drowning in regret usually take complete responsibility for a situation; they don't consider any other problems that contributed to the issue, particularly those outside of their control.

_____

_____

_____

_____

_____

_____

_____

_____

_____

_____

_____

_____

_____

_____

_____

_____

_____

_____

_____

_____

_____

_____

"Was there anything I did right in the situation that I can be proud of?"

We tend to focus exclusively on the negative, devastating aspects of a scenario.

Instead, try to remember the beauty too – however fleeting – and give this equal attention.

_____

_____

_____

_____

_____

_____

_____

_____

_____

_____

_____

_____

_____

_____

_____

_____

_____

_____

_____

_____

"As a result of this experience, have I adapted the way I behave and respond to similar situations?"

Most likely you'll find that you have learned substantial life lessons, and that you have acquired a sense of how to proceed hereafter.

Furthermore, we are kinder and more thoughtful humans if we can acknowledge the past and seek to improve.

"Is there anything I can do now that will make a difference about what I think and how I feel about the situation?"

It is humanly impossible to change the past...but there are countless ways we can grow into wiser, more considerate versions of ourselves.

In situations we cannot change, despite how much we want to, the most gracious thing we can do is to practice self-forgiveness.

_____
_____
_____
_____
_____
_____
_____
_____
_____
_____
_____
_____
_____
_____
_____
_____
_____
_____

Processing Grief: What Do I Do? How Do I Go On?

The words I share most often with those who are grieving the loss of their companion animals are "what's on the inside will always find a way out."

This means that our thoughts and our emotions – anything we stuff down in an attempt to make go away – will always find a way the surface. When they do bubble up, we need to establish healthy ways to cope.

The only way we move through grief is to experience all facets of it. There is no path to circumnavigate our heartbreak.

Below are suggestions and reflection questions for processing suppressed grief when it surfaces.

Suggestions & Reflection Questions:

Spend more time nurturing relationships you cherish, versus those you feel obligated to be in (i.e., people you actually like).

Who makes you feel "seen" when you're with them, and with whom you feel a connection?

Not sure who these people might be?

Quick test: Remember your last visit with a person. How did you feel after? Cared for and appreciated -- or drained and frazzled?

With whom can you be your true self – without pretentions or insincerity?

_____

_____

_____

_____

_____

_____

_____

_____

_____

_____

_____

_____

_____

_____

Holding things in – thoughts, emotions, words, behaviors – can exacerbate their intensity, which could result in impulsive decision-making when they do erupt.

What do you want to release in this moment, without judgement from yourself or anyone else, that would aid in your healing?

_____

_____

_____

_____

_____

_____

_____

_____

_____

_____

_____

_____

_____

_____

_____

_____

_____

_____

_____

_____

Sleep is essential for human functioning. Specifically, restorative sleep promotes rationale thought patterns, which can stave off distressing ruminations, anxiety, and destructive reactions.

Gentle reminder: once you are in bed, try not to use electronic devices, watch TV, check social media, or talk on the phone – all of which can distract from the body's natural progression for falling and staying asleep.

If you need to engage with the outside world once in bed, do so outside of the bedroom.

You can also place a notebook and pen on your nightstand, to write down any concerns that might keep you up. These can be dealt with in the morning.

What makes you want to go to bed? (fresh sheets, cozy pajamas, a warm bath or shower, a good book, warmer / cooler temperature?)

_____

_____

_____

_____

_____

_____

_____

_____

_____

_____

_____

_____

Schedule daily restorative activities (a walk, exercise, spending time outdoors, meditation), eat nutritious meals and snacks, and stay hydrated.

This is self-care, and you must prioritize your needs – yes these are needs, not wants – during this time.

What are your self-care needs during this time?

_____

_____

_____

_____

_____

_____

_____

_____

_____

_____

_____

_____

_____

_____

_____

_____

_____

_____

_____

_____

Fill a box of sentimental items, or create a vision board that inspires you – photos, art, fabric, dried flowers, letters, quotes, poems, travel souvenirs, newspaper clippings, and articles about concerns you care about.

We tend to forget who we are in grief – what we find beautiful, causes we have dedicated our lives to, what we find hope in.

A project like this reminds us that our heart continues to beat, despite being submerged in grief.

Who, what, and where does your heart beat for?

_____

_____

_____

_____

_____

_____

_____

_____

_____

_____

_____

_____

_____

_____

_____

_____

_____

_____

Make a list of activities that -- when you're doing them – you find yourself smiling, if only momentarily. (Please know I appreciate how challenging this request may be at this time).

This might include visiting a peaceful spot in nature, a museum, being in the company of animals, a weekend excursion, trying a new hobby, volunteering, or attending a sporting event.

When we are grieving, there is often an inclination to engage in behaviors that seem protective and ameliorating in the short-term, but which can actually worsen our moods. For example, staying in bed all day or binging TV may offer temporary "relief," but ultimately this lack of movement will only prolong our symptoms.

What will help is engaging in behavioral activation: thoughtfully and purposefully engaging in interests to evoke an improved mood.

My list of activities:

_____

_____

_____

_____

_____

_____

_____

_____

_____

_____

Consider what type of "help" you'd like, if any at all, when loved ones ask what they can do.

You may want them to spend time with you, run errands, drop off coffee, or have meals delivered to your home. If they are asking, it's absolutely ok to respond with what you'd actually appreciate.

It's also entirely alright to ask for time and space alone too.

What do you really want to ask for?

_____

_____

_____

_____

_____

_____

_____

_____

_____

_____

_____

_____

_____

_____

_____

_____

_____

You may want to remove anything from your home or phone that you might utilize in an attempt to self-soothe but later wish you hadn't (e.g., sweets, a cocktail, Amazon Prime). You can also ask trusted loved ones to do this for you.

The thought is if you don't have immediate access, the urge will pass, and you'll be grateful you didn't act on impulse.

What types of things offer you temporary satisfaction, but you ultimately wish you hadn't done?

_____

_____

_____

_____

_____

_____

_____

_____

_____

_____

_____

_____

_____

_____

_____

_____

_____

Moving Toward Acceptance

"You should be here with me."

I would venture to say that everyone who has lost their animal will tell you that they've had this longing at least once, if not constantly.

Often, this is accompanied by convictions such as "I didn't do enough for them while they were alive;" "they deserved so much more;" "they didn't know how much I loved them," or "it shouldn't be this way."

Try to imagine what a relief it would be – physically, mentally, and emotionally – to no longer carry the intense burden of these statements.

Accepting our loss involves two arduous but necessary steps: 1) letting go of any blameful judgments of ourselves, and 2) viewing reality as it actually is (the facts of the situation).

These can feel like an impossible ask of us. We may even feel selfish: if I accept what happened, I am exonerating myself for the role I played. I should be suffering – I don't deserve to be happy.

Or, for some of us, we hold on to the unbearable components of our loss because we believe if we let go, we're letting go of our bond.

Further still, some of us remain in mourning because we know what to expect from misery. Thus, we can feel some semblance of control. What we can't control is grief stealing our happiness again.

These beliefs couldn't be farther from the truth.

When we move toward acceptance, we are set free to treasure the relationship we shared with our animal, and find beauty in the memories we made.

These memories are ours forever, and nothing can take them away.

Reflection Questions:

Are there any rigid thoughts or invasive feelings that prevent you from accepting your loss?

_____

_____

_____

_____

_____

_____

_____

_____

_____

_____

_____

_____

_____

_____

_____

_____

_____

_____

_____

_____

_____

_____

_____

What would you tell a dear friend if they shared similar thoughts and feelings as what you wrote above?

_____

_____

_____

_____

_____

_____

_____

_____

_____

_____

_____

_____

_____

_____

_____

_____

_____

_____

_____

_____

_____

_____

How would you feel if you knew you had done absolutely everything within your power for your animal while they were physically here with you?

_____

_____

_____

_____

_____

_____

_____

_____

_____

_____

_____

_____

_____

_____

_____

_____

_____

_____

_____

_____

_____

_____

A Sacred Space to Release...and Return

This journal was written to provide solace, grace, and hope. A protective embrace. A gentle spot to land.

However, the path toward healing is unique for everyone. No two grief journeys are the same.

At this time, I would encourage you to consider if we haven't discussed the aspect(s) of grief that brought you here.

Below are prompts that invite you to speak to what hasn't already been shared.

Reflection Questions:

Are there elements of your loss that we have not touched on, but would be beneficial to bring to light?

_____

_____

_____

_____

_____

_____

_____

_____

_____

_____

_____

_____

_____

_____

_____

_____

_____

_____

_____

_____

_____

_____

Are there any questions you are hesitant to reflect on? Why might this be the case?

Is there something weighing heavy on your heart, your mind, your soul, your spirit -- that needs to be released?

Below is a sacred space to do just this...

_____

_____

_____

_____

_____

_____

_____

_____

_____

_____

_____

_____

_____

_____

_____

_____

_____

_____

_____

_____

My Parting Sentiments to You

I have often considered why we humans are drawn to – and love – animals.

Is it because they are our loyal companions, who touch our lives and teach us what it feels like to bond with another soul?

Is it because they demonstrate how to live in the present moments of life's unpredictable journey?

Is it because caring for them often involves putting their needs before our own, nurturing a more selfless, giving version of who we want to be?

Is it because they constantly forgive those who have let them down in the past, with a trusting tail wag, a soft purr, or a gentle nudge?

Is it because their affection expands our hearts, proving that love only makes us richer, the more we give it away?

Or is it because animals show us how to listen carefully, to patiently observe, and to respond with tenderness and respect?

I hope we can find consolation in the belief that our animals who have passed are now at peace, and their spirits continue to surround us.

Perhaps frolicking free from pain in vast meadows, basking in endless sunshine, or gazing over us from the skies above.

Let their legacy continue to guide our actions, as we strive to be better stewards of the natural world, ensuring that future generations can experience animals' existence with wonder.

May we continue to support one another through the healing process, extending compassion to all who have experienced the void of a profound loss.

And let the relationship we share as a community grow stronger, united by our dedication and devotion to protecting and caring for animals.

May their souls rest in perfect serenity.

Katie

✳✳✳

About The Author

Dr. Katie Lawlor

Katie Lawlor, Psy.D., MIA, received her doctorate from the joint program between the Stanford University Department of Psychiatry and Behavioral Sciences and the Pacific Graduate School of Psychology.

She trained at both the Stanford University Medical Center and the VA Palo Alto Health Care System, focusing on Cognitive Behavioral Therapy (CBT), neuropsychology, and human-animal interactions (HAI). Prior to her career in clinical psychology, Dr. Lawlor held positions with NBC News in New York City, the U.S. Department of State in Washington DC, and the Governor's Office of California.

Education & Training:

Clinical Internship, VA Northern California Health Care System
Psy.D., Clinical Psychology, PGSP-Stanford Consortium
M.I.A., Economic Policy, Columbia University
B.A., University of Notre Dame ☘

About the Editor

Dr. Dustin Kieschnick

Dustin Kieschnick, Psy.D. is a clinical psychologist who specializes in trauma and post-traumatic stress, grief and loss, and family and relational systems.

He is currently a Clinical Assistant Professor at the University of California, San Francisco (UCSF), and has worked as a consultant for start-up and corporate organizations on interpersonal communications, trauma in the workplace, and implementing trauma-informed practices. Dr. Kieschnick also served nine years as a United States Marine.

Education & Training:

Clinical Internship, Bronx VA, New York City
Psy.D., Clinical Psychology, PGSP-Stanford Consortium
B.A., University of Houston

Made in the USA
Columbia, SC
01 March 2024

fdb26c5d-a407-4a65-adc6-fb76dd612cbdR02